Assad Khan of

THE
BUBBLE
TEA
BOOK

50 Fun and Delicious Recipes for Love at First Sip!

EBURY
PRESS

CONTENTS

FOREWORD 4

BUBBLE TEA & ITS ORIGINS 6

THE ANATOMY OF BUBBLE TEA 7

  1: Soluble sweeteners 8

  2: Pearls 10

  3: The tea base 17

  4: Crowns 18

  Putting it all together 20

COLD BUBBLE TEAS
22

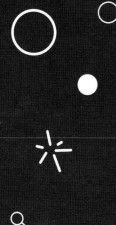

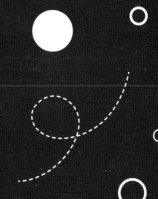

HOT MILK TEAS
46

ICED BLITZ SMOOTHIES & CREAM CROWNS
54

ADVANCED MIXOLOGY
62

BUBBLE TEA COCKTAILS & MOCKTAILS
86

INGREDIENTS GLOSSARY 108

EQUIPMENT GLOSSARY 109

INDEX 110

ACKNOWLEDGEMENTS 111

FOREWORD

My bubble tea story is one of love at first drink. I drank my first bubble tea in 2009 and fell in love with it. So much so that I left my career to learn the art of bubble tea in Taiwan, with the hope of launching my own brand. I never could have imagined where this exciting journey would take me or how my trajectory would change.

After months of learning and preparation, Bubbleology was born in Soho, London, in April 2011. I wanted to share the experience I'd had and the skills I'd mastered in Taiwan. The journey so far has been exciting and unexpected, and I want to thank the Bubbleology team, everyone around the world who has helped to grow the trend of drinking bubble tea and our loyal customers, who have supported us along the way.

'The joy of bubble tea comes from its unique taste, the variety of flavours, the texture of the pearls and its entirely customisable nature.'

In light of the fast growth of the bubble tea industry, I believe that now is the time to demystify the process of making these drinks at home. This bubble tea bible has been created to inspire a new generation of consumers: it is for anyone and everyone, whether you're new to bubble tea, a long-time fan of the beverage or an experienced mixologist looking for ways to include tapioca pearls in your drinks.

The book looks at every stage of the bubble tea process, from making the tapioca to different tea bases, mixology techniques and flavour varieties. The recipes have been inspired by Bubbleology's own drinks menu, and include drinks for all occasions, ranging from simple to advanced recipes, as well as cocktails and mocktails.

I hope you will enjoy exploring these recipes and experimenting with flavour combinations, becoming your own mixologist. Savour the flavours, tantalise your taste buds, experience new tastes and textures and discover your next drink obsession. Bubble tea is the drink you'll love to eat!

Assad Khan

CEO and Founder of Bubbleology

BUBBLE TEA & ITS ORIGINS

Bubble tea is a refreshing tea-based beverage containing tapioca pearls.
It is consumed using a fat straw, which is wide enough for the tapioca pearls to fit through. It comes in different flavours and a variety of tea bases can be used. There are both milk and fruit tea versions, and it can be consumed hot or cold, although it is traditionally served as a cold beverage.

This delicious drink originated in Taiwan in the early 1980s. Opinions differ about who first created bubble tea, but everyone can agree that, whoever it was, it was a genius creation.

Since its first humble incarnation as a plain tea base with tapioca pearls, bubble tea has been through an exciting evolution. It now has an extraordinary variety of flavours, as well as differing delicious and indulgent toppings.

Taipei

Taiwan

About Bubbleology

Bubbleology was born in the heart of Soho in 2011 and has since expanded across the UK and internationally. There is a long history behind bubble tea, and it is important to us to recognise its Taiwanese heritage. We are proud to do our part in bringing greater awareness to this iconic drink.

However, Bubbleology is not a traditional Taiwanese bubble tea offering, and we have taken our own unique approach to this amazing beverage. Our intention has always been to create an 'alternative' bubble tea experience, with exciting mixology approaches, unique dessert-drink fusions and even alcoholic bubble tea!

The recipes have been simplified to allow you to make bubble tea at home with ease. Certain ingredients have been amended to allow you to source them more easily, and are not the same as what would be used either in our stores or in Taiwan. Our aim here is clear: to simplify the experience of making bubble tea.

THE ANATOMY OF BUBBLE TEA

Bubble tea is all about mixology!
You can choose different tea bases, flavours, tapioca (even popping boba) and toppings. The choice is entirely yours, and you are your own mixologist. But, however you combine them, the principles remain the same: you must have a **tea base**, **pearls**, **flavourings** and a **soluble sweetener** – and, of course, a **bubble tea straw** to drink it through!

The following sections of the book will show you how to create these base elements so that you can start the mixology process.

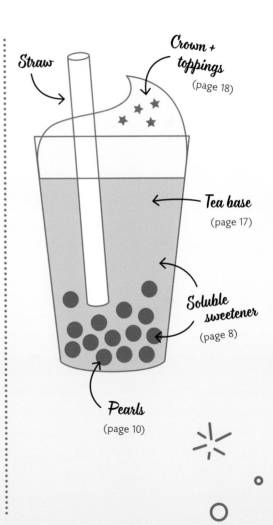

Straw

Crown + toppings
(page 18)

Tea base
(page 17)

Soluble sweetener
(page 8)

Pearls
(page 10)

Servings

All the recipes in this book make one serving, but you can easily scale up the quantities to make more!

1: SOLUBLE SWEETENERS

Bubble tea is a dessert drink most often consumed cold. It requires an immediately soluble sweetener (which is also used to sweeten the tapioca). There are many options that can be used, such as agave syrup, cane syrup or honey. Another popular solution is the 'simple syrup' opposite, which can be made at home (and is much cheaper than the other alternatives). We suggest that you start off with this method.

Sweetening bubble teas

The amount of soluble sweetener that you use in each of the bubble teas in this book is down to your own personal preference. We suggest that, for bubble teas in which the components do not add any additional sweetness to the drink (such as Assam or Jasmine milk teas), that you add 10–30ml (2 teaspoons–2 tablespoons) of simple syrup to a 500ml (18fl oz) serving. However, you may need to reduce this quantity, or leave it out

completely, for recipes that use ingredients such as fruit puree, which will naturally add sweetness to the drink base. For this reason, we always suggest you taste the mixture before adding the sweetener so that you can make a judgement on how much to add.

SIMPLE SYRUP

You will require a larger amount of 'simple syrup' than you might expect, as it is also used to sweeten the tapioca. It can be stored for later use – it will keep in the fridge for a couple of weeks.

MAKES ABOUT 300ML (10FL OZ)
– enough for one batch of tapioca
   plus around ten drinks

YOU WILL NEED:
– 180ml (6fl oz) water
– 340g (12oz) caster (superfine) sugar

EQUIPMENT:
– scales
– small saucepan
– metal strainer or sieve
– heatproof jug
– bottle with pourable spout

Put the measured water into a small saucepan over a high heat and bring it to the boil. Once the water has reached boiling point, slowly add the sugar. Stir constantly until the sugar has fully dissolved, then turn off the heat and allow the solution to cool for at least 5 minutes (but ensure that the solution does not go cold).

Pour the sugar syrup through a strainer or sieve and into the heatproof jug. Let the syrup cool, then pour it into a bottle with an easily pourable spout. This solution can be used to sweeten both the tapioca and the bubble teas when required.

Or try this:

– Replace the caster sugar with coconut sugar or other variants.

– If you really want to spice things up, add a stick of cinnamon or a piece of star anise to the syrup to infuse it with flavour.

2: PEARLS

PERFECT TAPIOCA

This is an essential component: getting the tapioca right is the key to making the perfect bubble tea.

There are two distinct stages to cooking the perfect tapioca, and both are equally important! So make sure you follow the recipe closely. This recipe is based on tapioca that requires a total cooking time of 1 hour. Please check the packet instructions of your tapioca and adjust the timings if needed.

MAKES ABOUT 1.7KG (3LB 12OZ)
– enough for 18 servings

YOU WILL NEED:
– 3 litres (5¼ pints) water
– 1kg (2lb 4oz) raw tapioca pearls
– 100g (3½oz) caster (superfine) sugar
– 75–100ml (2½–3½fl oz) soluble
  sweetener (Simple syrup, page 9,
  agave syrup or cane syrup)

EQUIPMENT:
– scales
– large saucepan
– plastic colander
– metal colander

Stage one

Pour the measured water into the saucepan. Place over a high heat and bring to the boil. While the water is warming up, weigh out the tapioca pearls and pour into the plastic colander. Shake gently over a bin in order to remove any small debris until there is none left.

Once the water is boiling, slowly add the tapioca to the saucepan. Stir for about a minute to ensure that the tapioca pearls are separated and not stuck together or to the bottom of the pot.

Cover with a lid and leave to simmer for 30 minutes over a low heat. Stir the tapioca occasionally to ensure the pearls don't stick together, and always keep the lid on between stirring. After 30 minutes, take out a small spoonful of pearls and put them in a cup of iced water. Leave them for 30 seconds to cool, then stir and taste them. The core of the pearls should be soft – if they are still hard in the centre, allow a further 5 minutes of cooking time and test again. When the centre of the pearls is soft, you can move on to stage two.

Stage two

Reduce the heat to a very gentle simmer – it is critical to ensure that the heat is very low, allowing for a gentle cooking process. Add the sugar and stir gently. Cover and simmer very gently for 20–25 minutes, stirring regularly.

After 20–25 minutes take out a small spoonful of tapioca and put it into a cup of iced water. Stir and taste. Not all raw tapioca is the same, so you need to test it to ensure that the tapioca is the perfect consistency for you. If it needs longer, continue cooking at a gentle simmer for another 5 minutes, then test again. Continue until you have that perfect soft, chewy consistency.

Once the tapioca is perfect, strain into the metal colander. Rinse with cold water to ensure any further debris is removed, stirring as you rinse. Now transfer the tapioca to a bowl or other container. Stir in your preferred sweetener (we suggest our Simple syrup on page 9 for those new to bubble tea), according to your taste preference. The tapioca will not keep, so you must use it within about 4 hours.

CARAMELISED TAPIOCA

This is a delicious variant, which has a caramelised taste and velvety texture. It is always served warm. There are many variations to try: this is just one suggestion to kick-start your creativity! It uses exactly the same method for the first stage (see page 11), but the second stage is different and there is an additional third stage. You will need to use a soup kettle/soup warmer or a similar piece of equipment, as the tapioca must be kept constantly warm at around 65°C (150°F).

MAKES ABOUT 1.8KG (4LB)
– enough for 18 servings

YOU WILL NEED:
– 1 batch tapioca which has been
   cooked to first stage only (page 11)
– 1 litre (1¾ pints) boiling water
– 350g (12oz) soft dark brown sugar
– 40ml (3 tbsp) molasses or
   black treacle

EQUIPMENT:
– jug
– large saucepan
– colander
– soup kettle/soup warmer or similar

Stage one

Complete stage one of the tapioca cooking procedure (page 11), then turn the heat off. Leave the tapioca in the pan.

Stage two

Pour the measured boiling water into a jug, then add 100g (3½oz) of the dark brown sugar. Stir until the sugar is fully dissolved. Slowly pour this brown sugar solution into the tapioca saucepan and stir until it is evenly distributed. Cover with the lid and gently simmer for around 20–25 minutes, stirring on a regular basis.

Meanwhile, get the soup kettle ready. Put 150g (5½oz) of the brown sugar into the soup kettle and turn it to a high heat to soften.

When the tapioca's simmering time is up, take out a spoonful of pearls, cool them in a cup of iced water, then taste to ensure they are soft. Once you are happy, drain the tapioca into a colander over the sink, but **do not** rinse it – it must remain warm, and keep all the softened debris around it!

Stage three

Immediately pour the still-warm tapioca into the soup kettle – do not allow it to cool! By now the sugar you added to the soup kettle should have softened, so stir it into the tapioca, then add the remaining 100g (3½oz) brown sugar and mix again. Add the molasses or black treacle for extra flavour and stir through.

Close the lid of the soup kettle and wait 5 minutes before serving. It is crucial that you leave the soup kettle on to keep the tapioca at a temperature of about 65°C (150°F).

Or try this:

– There are many different varieties of tapioca – feel free to experiment and enjoy the delights of differing pearls and textures!

– Caramelised tapioca can use a variety of differing sugar types. Honey can also be added if desired. You can add other flavour bases to the tapioca after you have cooked it as well, so go ahead and experiment!

POPPING BOBA & NATA DE COCO

Traditional tapioca is not the only delicious element of bubble tea that can be sucked up through the oversized straw: you can also use popping boba, nata de coco and even chia seeds!

This book's recipes will focus on tapioca, as well as popping boba and nata de coco.

POPPING BOBA

Unlike tapioca, popping boba has a thin, gel-like skin made from a seaweed extract, and juice inside that bursts out or 'pops' when the round pearls are squeezed. It's 100 per cent vegan.

NATA DE COCO

A coconut gel. This is a chewy, translucent, jelly-like food produced by the fermentation of coconut water. The flavoured variety is commonly used in bubble teas. It's 100 per cent vegan.

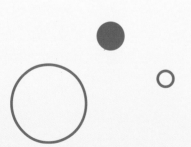

3: THE TEA BASE

The other key component of a good bubble tea is the tea base, which can be made from many different varieties of tea. The recipes in this book will focus purely on Jasmine and Assam tea. If you are using Assam, you will need to brew it to be much stronger than usual (we recommend brewing it for around two or three times longer than recommended on the packet), as darker teas like Assam require their full flavour to come out. However, you should not do this with Jasmine tea, otherwise it will become very bitter. Always ensure that you brew Jasmine tea according to the packet instructions.

We recommend brewing a large quantity of tea, so that you can make multiple drinks.

Tips:

– The tea should always be poured into a pre-warmed Thermos unless you're using it immediately, as it needs to be warm when it's added to the bubble tea. Jasmine and Assam teas should be held in the Thermos for a maximum of two hours as they will degrade over time.

– Jasmine tea should always be brewed at a temperature of 70–75°C (158–167°F). Brewing it at too high a temperature could lead to bitterness.

– Ensure that you use the best strainer possible when decanting the tea, as you don't want any sediment left in it (this would cause bitterness).

– Never over-brew Jasmine tea, and constantly taste it as you go to make sure you're happy with the flavour.

– It is completely normal for your Assam tea to taste very strong, as it needs to be able to cut through the taste of the milk and add body to the drink.

– Experiment with other tea bases, such as Oolong, Earl Grey or Chamomile!

– For a single serving, you can just use a basic tea bag and boiling water from a kettle.

4: CROWNS

Note: If you are making bubble tea for the first time, our suggestion would be to skip this part and come back to it once you are comfortable with the basic process and making some of the more simple flavours.

Bubble tea isn't just about the pearls. It can also have delicious 'crowns', which come in many varieties! You'll be spoilt for choice, trying to decide whether to suck and chew the pearls first, or gently sip and consume the crown along with the drink base!

Cream crown

The crown that we will be focusing on in this book is a salted cream cheese variety, but remember that these creations are limited only by your imagination. Our job is to get you experimenting; your job is to keep playing with new varieties and to create your own mixology!

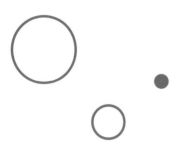

MAKES 750ML (1¼ PINTS)
– enough for 10 servings

YOU WILL NEED:
– 1 tbsp cream cheese
– pinch of Himalayan pink salt
– 300ml (½ pint) double (heavy) cream
– 300ml (½ pint) organic full-fat milk, plus a splash

EQUIPMENT:
– large mixing jug
– handheld electric whisk
– spatula

Put the cream cheese into the mixing jug with a pinch of Himalayan pink salt and a small splash of milk. Mix thoroughly using a handheld electric whisk, ensuring there are no lumps.

Pour in the double cream and whisk again until well combined.

Once combined, gradually add the milk, folding it in with a spatula. Be careful to not add all the milk at the same time. The mixture should be thick and fluffy. You can now use the salted cream cheese mix as a topping or 'crown' for your bubble tea.

Or try this:

– Try experimenting by adding other flavour bases to the mixture.

– You can colour the toppings using natural food colouring or add another layer of decorative garnish on top of the crown when you place it on to the finished bubble tea.

– If you feel particularly indulgent, you can add a scoop of gelato to the top of your favourite bubble tea in place of the cream crown to create an exciting float!

19

PUTTING IT ALL TOGETHER

Now that you know how to create tapioca, tea bases and a cream crown topping, you will be able to put your bubble tea together.

In general, the principles of crafting a bubble tea are first to add the pearls to the base of the glass, then to pour over the flavoured tea blend. Then, depending on the drink, you can add any toppings or crowns.

On the following pages we have suggestions for fruit teas, milk teas, indulgent exotic combinations and even alcoholic varieties. We believe that there is no one way to create a bubble tea – you are your own mixologist! It's all about the way you want to make the drink, so never be afraid to evolve the drink to your own tastes, or even to amend the suggested recipes in the book!

BEFORE YOU BEGIN:

Always adjust to your taste!

We have taken great care to try and simplify the ingredient components in this book as much as possible, as we understand that certain elements may be unfamiliar to those who have never experienced bubble tea before. Every flavour base (such as fruit purees or dried ingredients) will have differing strength, sweetness and viscosity levels. So, we suggest that you follow the dosing instructions on the ingredient labels, and if you need to adjust the strength of the flavour, simply increase or decrease where required. You can then adjust the sweetness accordingly using the suggested soluble sweeteners. Each bubble tea is all about you. Make the drink according to your preference – the only right way to make the drink is the way you love to drink it!

MILKS

For the drinks that require milk, the type of milk you use is also entirely up to you. The drink can taste very different depending on the type of milk that you choose. We are big fans of plant-based milks, but just remember that each type will have a different flavour and so affect the flavour of the bubble tea. The recipes in this book assume the use of organic, full-fat milk, so do bear this in mind if you use other choices of milk. We do not recommend the use of diluted milk types, such as skimmed milk, as it will make your drinks watery.

MEASUREMENTS & SHAKERS

Please note that the mixology of these drinks uses a 500ml (18fl oz) cocktail shaker, and it's important that you keep to this size when mixing as the ingredient components and instructions have been calibrated accordingly.

The exact amount of tea or other liquid you need to add to your recipes may vary depending on the size of your ice cubes and the other ingredients. To keep things simple, we have not given precise measurements for some of these quantities, and instead you will see 'to fill'. This means that, once you've put all your other ingredients in the 500ml (18fl oz) shaker, you simply need to fill it to the top with the tea or other specified liquid and you'll get the results you're after.

Remember:

The only right way to make the drink is the way you love to drink it!

COLD BUBBLE TEAS

Most bubble teas are consumed cold, even in the colder winter months! In this chapter you will find a selection of some basic cold bubble teas for you to try at home. They are the perfect starting point for you to learn how to make bubble tea. All of these drinks assume 'full ice', meaning that the shakers are filled to the brim with ice – if you prefer less ice, just compensate by using more of the drink base.

ASSAM MILK TEA

YOU WILL NEED:
- 100ml (3½fl oz) organic full-fat milk (or milk of your choice, see page 21)
- ice
- freshly brewed Assam tea (page 17), to fill
- about 20ml (4 tsp) soluble sweetener, such as agave syrup, cane syrup or Simple syrup (page 9), or to taste
- 1 ladleful tapioca (page 10) or caramelised tapioca (page 12)

EQUIPMENT:
- 500ml (18fl oz) cocktail shaker
- 500ml (18fl oz) serving glass
- pea ladle
- bubble tea straw

Pour the milk into the shaker. Fill the shaker with ice and pour in the freshly brewed Assam tea until the shaker is full almost to the brim. Put the lid on and shake for a few seconds. Taste for sweetness and add the soluble sweetener to taste, then shake again.

Put your chosen tapioca pearls into the base of your serving glass and pour over the contents of the shaker. Serve.

Or try this:

Experiment with other dark tea flavours, such as Oolong or even Earl Grey tea.

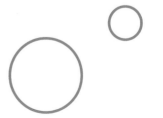

TARO MILK TEA

YOU WILL NEED:
- freshly brewed Jasmine tea (page 17), to fill
- 100 per cent pure dried taro powder (check packet instructions for quantity, or to taste)
- 100ml (3½fl oz) organic full-fat milk (or milk of your choice, see page 21)
- ice
- about 20ml (4 tsp) soluble sweetener, such as agave syrup, cane syrup or Simple syrup (page 9), or to taste
- about 1 ladleful tapioca (page 10) or caramelised tapioca (page 12)

EQUIPMENT:
- blender
- 500ml (18fl oz) cocktail shaker
- 500ml (18fl oz) serving glass
- pea ladle
- bubble tea straw

Pour 80ml (2¾fl oz) of the freshly brewed Jasmine tea into the blender. Add the taro powder and milk and blend until combined.

Fill the shaker with ice and add the blended taro mix. Top up with more Jasmine tea until the shaker is full almost to the brim. Put the lid on and shake for a few seconds. Taste for sweetness and add the soluble sweetener to taste, then shake again.

Put your chosen tapioca pearls into the base of your serving glass and pour over the contents of the shaker. Serve.

Or try this:

For ease of mixology, we have suggested using 100 per cent pure organic dried taro powder. However, you could also use freshly cooked taro or precooked, canned taro – that is, of course, if you are feeling adventurous!

JASMINE MILK TEA

YOU WILL NEED:
- 100ml (3½fl oz) organic full-fat milk (or milk of your choice, see page 21)
- ice
- freshly brewed Jasmine tea (page 17), to fill
- about 20ml (4 tsp) soluble sweetener, such as agave syrup, cane syrup or Simple syrup (page 9), or to taste
- about 1 ladleful tapioca (page 10) or caramelised tapioca (page 12)

EQUIPMENT:
- 500ml (18fl oz) cocktail shaker
- 500ml (18fl oz) serving glass
- pea ladle
- bubble tea straw

Pour the milk into the shaker. Fill the shaker with ice and pour in the freshly brewed Jasmine tea until the shaker is full almost to the brim. Put the lid on and shake for a few seconds. Taste for sweetness and add the soluble sweetener to taste, then shake again.

Put your chosen tapioca pearls into the base of your serving glass and pour over the contents of the shaker. Serve.

Or try this:

Experiment with other green tea flavours. You could even try experimenting with herbal teas, such as Chamomile.

MATCHA MILK TEA

YOU WILL NEED:
- freshly brewed Jasmine tea (page 17), to fill
- ½ tsp pure matcha powder (see tip)
- 100ml (3½fl oz) organic full-fat milk (or milk of your choice, see page 21)
- ice
- about 30ml (2 tbsp) soluble sweetener, such as agave syrup, cane syrup or Simple syrup (page 9), or to taste
- about 1 ladleful tapioca (page 10) or caramelised tapioca (page 12)

EQUIPMENT:
- blender
- 500ml (18fl oz) cocktail shaker
- 500ml (18fl oz) serving glass
- pea ladle
- bubble tea straw

Pour 80ml (2¾fl oz) of the freshly brewed Jasmine tea into the blender. Add the matcha powder and milk and blend until combined.

Fill the shaker with ice and add the matcha mix. Top up with more Jasmine tea until the shaker is full almost to the brim. Put the lid on and shake for a few seconds. Taste for sweetness and add the soluble sweetener to taste, then shake again.

Put your chosen tapioca pearls into the base of your serving glass and pour over the contents of the shaker. Serve.

Top tip
Be careful to follow the label instructions when dosing the matcha powder, as you won't need as much as you think!

COCONUT MILK TEA

YOU WILL NEED:
- freshly brewed Jasmine tea (page 17), to fill
- coconut milk powder (check packet instructions for quantity, or to taste)
- 100ml (3½fl oz) organic full-fat milk (or milk of your choice, see page 21)
- ice
- about 20ml (4 tsp) soluble sweetener, such as agave syrup, cane syrup or Simple syrup (page 9), or to taste
- about 1 ladleful tapioca (page 10) or caramelised tapioca (page 12)

EQUIPMENT:
- blender
- 500ml (18fl oz) cocktail shaker
- 500ml (18fl oz) serving glass
- pea ladle
- bubble tea straw

Pour 80ml (2¾fl oz) of the freshly brewed Jasmine tea into the blender. Add the coconut milk powder and milk and blend until combined.

Fill the shaker with ice and add the blended coconut mix. Top up with more Jasmine tea until the shaker is full almost to the brim. Put the lid on and shake for a few seconds. Taste for sweetness and add the soluble sweetener to taste, then shake again.

Put your chosen tapioca pearls into the base of your serving glass and pour over the contents of the shaker. Serve.

Or try this:

Try using pure coconut milk instead of dairy milk and coconut milk powder in this recipe.

PASSION FRUIT TEA

YOU WILL NEED:

- freshly brewed Jasmine tea
  (page 17), to fill
- pulp of 2 fresh passion fruit
  (or passion fruit puree, to taste)
- ice
- about 30ml (2 tbsp) soluble
  sweetener, such as agave syrup, cane
  syrup or Simple syrup (page 9), or to
  taste
- about 1 ladleful tapioca (page 10),
  nata de coco or popping boba

EQUIPMENT:

- blender
- 500ml (18fl oz) cocktail shaker
- 500ml (18fl oz) serving glass
- pea ladle
- bubble tea straw

Pour 200ml (7fl oz) of the freshly brewed Jasmine tea into the blender. Add the passion fruit pulp or puree and blend until combined.

Fill the shaker with ice and add the blended passion fruit mix. Top up with more Jasmine tea until the shaker is full almost to the brim. Put the lid on and shake for a few seconds. Taste for sweetness and add the soluble sweetener to taste, then shake again.

Put the cooked tapioca pearls, nata de coco or popping boba into the base of your serving glass and pour over the contents of the shaker. Serve.

MANGO FRUIT TEA

YOU WILL NEED:
- freshly brewed Jasmine tea (page 17), to fill
- handful of diced mango (or mango puree, to taste)
- ice
- about 20ml (4 tsp) soluble sweetener, such as agave syrup, cane syrup or Simple syrup (page 9), or to taste
- about 1 ladleful tapioca (page 10), nata de coco or popping boba

EQUIPMENT:
- blender
- 500ml (18fl oz) cocktail shaker
- 500ml (18fl oz) serving glass
- pea ladle
- bubble tea straw

Pour 200ml (7fl oz) of the freshly brewed Jasmine tea into the blender. Add the diced mango or mango puree and blend until combined.

Fill the shaker with ice and add the blended mango mix. Top up with more Jasmine tea until the shaker is full almost to the brim. Put the lid on and shake for a few seconds. Taste for sweetness and add the soluble sweetener to taste, then shake again.

Put the cooked tapioca pearls, nata de coco or popping boba into the base of your serving glass and pour over the contents of the shaker. Serve.

STRAWBERRY FRUIT TEA

YOU WILL NEED:
- freshly brewed Jasmine tea (page 17), to fill
- handful of fresh strawberries (or strawberry puree, to taste)
- ice
- about 20ml (4 tsp) soluble sweetener, such as agave syrup, cane syrup or Simple syrup (page 9), or to taste
- about 1 ladleful tapioca (page 10), nata de coco or popping boba

EQUIPMENT:
- blender
- 500ml (18fl oz) cocktail shaker
- 500ml (18fl oz) serving glass
- pea ladle
- bubble tea straw

Pour 200ml (7fl oz) of the freshly brewed Jasmine tea into the blender. Add the strawberries or strawberry puree and blend until combined.

Fill the shaker with ice and add the blended strawberry mix. Top up with more Jasmine tea until the shaker is full almost to the brim. Put the lid on and shake for a few seconds. Taste for sweetness and add the soluble sweetener to taste, then blend again.

Put the cooked tapioca pearls, nata de coco or popping boba into the base of your serving glass and pour over the contents of the shaker. Serve.

ELECTRIC YUZU

YOU WILL NEED:
- pure yuzu puree, to taste
- about 1 ladleful tapioca (page 10), nata de coco or popping boba
- 50ml (2fl oz) freshly brewed Jasmine tea (page 17)
- lemonade, to fill
- natural blue food colouring (check packet instructions for quantity)

EQUIPMENT:
- 500ml (18fl oz) serving glass
- pea ladle
- bubble tea straw

Although this looks complicated, it's actually quite a simple drink! First, add a layer of yuzu puree to the bottom of the serving glass – the layer should be no more than 2.5cm (1 inch) thick. Add a layer of tapioca pearls, nata de coco or popping boba on top of the yuzu puree, then fill the glass with ice.

Pour the freshly brewed Jasmine tea over the top, then fill the remainder of the glass with lemonade. Add a few drops of natural blue food colouring for that iconic effect!

Top tip
Stir the bubble tea with your straw before you consume, so that the drink is infused with yuzu flavour.

SPICED CHAI TEA

YOU WILL NEED:
- ice
- 100ml (3½fl oz) organic full-fat milk (or milk of your choice, see page 21)
- freshly brewed spiced Chai tea, to fill
- about 20ml (4 tsp) soluble sweetener, such as agave syrup, cane syrup or Simple syrup (page 9), or to taste
- about 1 ladleful tapioca (page 10), or caramelised tapioca
- 1 cinnamon stick
- 2 star anise

EQUIPMENT:
- 500ml (18fl oz) cocktail shaker
- 500ml (18fl oz) serving glass
- pea ladle
- bubble tea straw

Fill the shaker to the brim with ice, then add the milk. Finally, pour in the freshly brewed spiced Chai tea until the shaker is full almost to the brim. Put the lid on and shake for a few seconds. Taste for sweetness and add the soluble sweetener to taste, then shake again.

Put your chosen tapioca pearls into the base of your serving glass, along with the cinnamon stick and star anise. Pour the Chai mix over the top and serve.

39

STRAWBERRY & MINT FIZZ

YOU WILL NEED:
- handful of strawberries (or strawberry puree, to taste)
- 100ml (3½fl oz) freshly brewed Jasmine tea (page 17)
- about 20ml (4 tsp) soluble sweetener, such as agave syrup, cane syrup or Simple syrup (page 9), or to taste
- a few fresh mint leaves, plus extra to garnish
- ice
- about 1 ladleful tapioca (page 10), nata de coco or popping boba
- lemonade, to fill

EQUIPMENT:

- blender
- 500ml (18fl oz) cocktail shaker
- muddler
- 500ml (18fl oz) serving glass
- pea ladle
- bubble tea straw

Put the strawberries or strawberry puree in the blender along with the freshly brewed Jasmine tea. Blend to combine.

Put the mint leaves in the shaker and use the muddler to crush them. Now fill the shaker with ice to the brim and pour in the blended strawberry mix. Put the lid on and shake for a few seconds. (The shaker will not be as full as in the previous recipes, but this is intentional.) Taste for sweetness and add the soluble sweetener to taste, then shake again.

Put the tapioca pearls, nata de coco or popping boba into the base of your serving glass, then pour in the contents of the shaker. Finally, top up the glass with your favourite lemonade, and garnish with fresh mint leaves.

Or try this:

Try swapping the lemonade for your favourite carbonated drink.

40

CARAMEL FRAPPE

YOU WILL NEED:
- 100ml (3½fl oz) freshly brewed black coffee
- 1 shot caramel syrup (check label for quantity, or to taste)
- organic full-fat milk (or milk of your choice, see page 21), to fill
- about 20ml (4 tsp) soluble sweetener, such as agave syrup, cane syrup or Simple syrup (page 9), or to taste
- about 1 ladleful tapioca (page 10), caramelised tapioca (page 12) or coffee-flavoured nata de coco
- whipped cream and toffee sauce, to finish

EQUIPMENT:
- 500ml (18fl oz) cocktail shaker
- 500ml (18fl oz) serving glass
- pea ladle
- bubble tea straw

Pour the freshly brewed coffee into the shaker along with the caramel syrup. Fill the shaker with ice, then fill almost to the brim with milk, put the lid on and shake for a few seconds. Taste for sweetness and add the soluble sweetener to taste, then shake again.

Put your chosen tapioca pearls or nata de coco into the serving glass and pour in the contents of the shaker. Top with whipped cream and drizzle with toffee sauce for that perfect 'pick me up'!

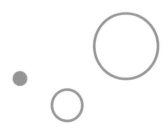

KEFIR & PINEAPPLE TEA

YOU WILL NEED:
- 50ml (2fl oz) milk kefir
- 120ml (4fl oz) pineapple juice
- ice
- freshly brewed Jasmine tea (page 17), to fill
- about 1 ladleful tapioca (page 10) or caramelised tapioca (page 12)
- slice of fresh pineapple, to serve

EQUIPMENT:
- 500ml (18fl oz) cocktail shaker
- 500ml (18fl oz) serving glass
- pea ladle
- bubble tea straw

Put the kefir and pineapple juice into the shaker. Fill the shaker with ice, then pour in the freshly brewed Jasmine tea until the shaker is full to the brim. Put the lid on and shake for a few seconds.

Put your chosen tapioca pearls into the base of the serving glass and pour in the kefir and pineapple mixture. Garnish with a slice of pineapple on the side of the glass and serve.

About kefir

Kefir is a fermented drink, traditionally made by adding kefir grains to cow's or goat's milk. It's a source of many nutrients!

43

JASMINE MILK TEA
WITH CARAMELISED
TAPIOCA

YOU WILL NEED:
- 100ml (3½fl oz) organic full-fat milk (or milk of your choice, see page 21)
- ice
- freshly brewed Jasmine tea (see page 17), to fill
- about 15ml (1 tbsp) soluble sweetener, such as agave syrup, cane syrup or Simple syrup (page 9), or to taste
- about 1 ladleful caramelised tapioca (page 12), plus sauce

EQUIPMENT:
- 500ml (18fl oz) cocktail shaker
- 500ml (18fl oz) serving glass
- pea ladle
- bubble tea straw

Put the milk into the shaker and fill the shaker with ice, then pour in the freshly brewed Jasmine tea until the shaker is full almost to the brim. Put the lid on and shake for a few seconds. Taste for sweetness and add the soluble sweetener to taste, then shake again.

Put the warm caramelised tapioca pearls into the base of the serving glass. Use a spoon to drizzle the caramelised sauce from the soup kettle around the inside of the glass. This will help create a distinctive 'striped' effect when pouring in the drink mix. Now slowly pour the contents of the shaker into the glass and serve.

Important!

The caramelised tapioca must always be kept warm in the soup kettle! The mixture of warm and cold in the drink creates an amazing sensation.

HOT MILK TEAS

Hot bubble teas are just as delectable as cold bubble teas. In this chapter you will find a selection of some hot bubble tea recipes that will keep your belly warm in those cold winter months!

HOT GINGER MILK TEA

YOU WILL NEED:
- organic full-fat milk (or milk of your choice, see page 21), to fill
- 100ml (3½fl oz) freshly brewed Assam tea (see page 17)
- ginger syrup (see packet instructions for quantity, or to taste)
- about 30ml (2 tbsp) soluble sweetener, such as agave syrup, cane syrup or Simple syrup (page 9), or to taste
- about 1 ladleful tapioca (page 10) or caramelised tapioca (page 12)

EQUIPMENT:
- small saucepan
- spoon
- 500ml (18fl oz) cocktail shaker
- 500ml (18fl oz) serving glass
- pea ladle
- bubble tea straw

Heat the milk in a small saucepan over a medium heat, but don't let it boil.

Put the freshly brewed Assam tea in the shaker along with the ginger syrup and stir. Then slowly pour in the hot milk until the shaker is full almost to the brim, stirring all the while (do not shake hot teas). Taste for sweetness and add the soluble sweetener to taste, then stir again.

Put your chosen tapioca pearls into the base of the serving glass, then pour the hot ginger milk tea mix over the top and serve.

Or try this:

Top with whipped cream and a miniature gingerbread man if you're feeling playful!

HOT COCOA
MILK TEA

YOU WILL NEED:
- organic full-fat milk (or milk of your choice, see page 21), to fill
- 60ml (4 tbsp) freshly brewed Jasmine tea (see page 17)
- pure cocoa powder (see packet instructions for quantity, or to taste), plus extra to garnish
- about 20ml (4 tsp) soluble sweetener, such as agave syrup, cane syrup or Simple syrup (page 9), or to taste
- about 1 ladleful tapioca (page 10) or caramelised tapioca (page 12)

EQUIPMENT:
- small saucepan
- spoon
- 500ml (18fl oz) cocktail shaker
- 500ml (18fl oz) serving glass
- pea ladle
- bubble tea straw

Heat the milk in a small saucepan over a medium heat, but don't let it boil.

Put the freshly brewed Jasmine tea in the shaker, along with the cocoa powder. Mix with a spoon until the contents are smooth and do not clump. Then slowly pour in the hot milk until the shaker is full almost to the brim, stirring all the while (do not shake hot teas). Taste for sweetness and add the soluble sweetener to taste, then stir again.

Put your chosen tapioca pearls into the base of the serving glass, then pour the contents of the shaker over the top. Garnish with cocoa powder and serve.

Or try this:

- Try adding mint or orange flavouring.

- Top with whipped cream and sprinkle with chocolate curls for extra indulgence.

HOT MATCHA LATTE

YOU WILL NEED:
- organic full-fat milk (or milk of your choice, see page 21), to fill
- ½ tsp pure matcha powder
- 50ml (2fl oz) warm water
- about 1 ladleful tapioca (page 10) or caramelised tapioca (page 12)
- about 40ml (3 tbsp) soluble sweetener, such as agave syrup, cane syrup or Simple syrup (page 9), or to taste

EQUIPMENT:
- small saucepan
- matcha bowl
- matcha whisk
- 500ml (18fl oz) serving glass
- pea ladle
- bubble tea straw

Heat the milk in a small saucepan over a medium heat, but don't let it boil.

Put the matcha powder into the matcha bowl. Add the warm water and whisk until smooth.

Put your chosen tapioca pearls into the base of the serving glass, then fill the glass almost to the top with hot milk. Pour the matcha mixture into the glass so that the green mixture slowly filters down into the warm milk. Taste for sweetness and add the soluble sweetener to taste, then gently stir.

Add a small sprinkle of the pure matcha on top to garnish, then serve.

HOT ASSAM TEA

YOU WILL NEED:
- organic full-fat milk (or milk of your choice, see page 21), to fill
- 180ml (6fl oz) freshly brewed Assam tea (see page 17)
- about 20ml (4 tsp) soluble sweetener, such as agave syrup, cane syrup or Simple syrup (page 9), or to taste
- about 1 ladleful tapioca (page 10) or caramelised tapioca (page 12)

EQUIPMENT:
- small saucepan
- spoon
- 500ml (18fl oz) cocktail shaker
- 500ml (18fl oz) serving glass
- pea ladle
- bubble tea straw

Heat the milk in a small saucepan over a medium heat, but don't let it boil.

Put the freshly brewed Assam tea in the shaker, then slowly pour in the hot milk until the shaker is full almost to the brim, stirring all the while (do not shake hot teas). Taste for sweetness and add the soluble sweetener to taste, then stir again.

Put your chosen tapioca pearls into the base of the serving glass and pour the Assam tea mix over the top. Serve.

Or try this:

Try out other hot tea flavours, such as Oolong tea – they are equally delicious.

HOT VANILLA CHAI MILK TEA

YOU WILL NEED:
- 100ml (3½fl oz) organic full-fat milk (or milk of your choice, see page 21)
- a few drops of vanilla extract (check packet instructions for exact quantity)
- freshly brewed spiced Chai tea, to fill
- about 30ml (2 tbsp) soluble sweetener, such as agave syrup, cane syrup or Simple syrup (page 9), or to taste
- about 1 ladleful tapioca (page 10) or caramelised tapioca (page 12)
- 3 cardamom pods, lightly crushed
- ground cinnamon, to garnish

EQUIPMENT:
- small saucepan
- spoon
- 500ml (18fl oz) cocktail shaker
- 500ml (18fl oz) serving glass
- pea ladle
- bubble tea straw

Heat the milk in a small saucepan over a medium heat, but don't let it boil.

Pour the hot milk into the shaker, along with the vanilla extract, and stir with a spoon. Gradually add the hot spiced Chai tea until the shaker is full almost to the brim, continuing to stir as you do so (do not shake hot teas). Taste for sweetness and add the soluble sweetener to taste, then stir again.

Put your chosen tapioca pearls into the base of the serving glass along with the cardamom pods, then pour the hot vanilla Chai blend over the top. Garnish with a sprinkling of ground cinnamon and serve. This is a perfect drink for those colder days!

ICED BLITZ SMOOTHIES & CREAM CROWNS

Try a delicious blended iced blitz smoothie to cool you down on those hot summer days! You will need xanthan gum, which is the secret to a great smoothie. It's a vegan thickening agent, which also helps prevent separation. You'll also find some bubble teas with cream crowns in this chapter.

MANGO
ICED BLITZ

YOU WILL NEED:
- handful of diced fresh mango (or mango puree, to taste)
- 100ml (3½fl oz) freshly brewed Jasmine tea (see page 17)
- ¼ tsp xanthan gum
- ice
- about 20ml (4 tsp) soluble sweetener, such as agave syrup, cane syrup or Simple syrup (page 9), or to taste
- about 1 ladleful tapioca (page 10), nata de coco or popping boba

EQUIPMENT:
- blender
- 500ml (18fl oz) cocktail shaker
- 500ml (18fl oz) serving glass
- pea ladle
- bubble tea straw

Put the diced mango or puree into the blender, along with the freshly brewed Jasmine tea and xanthan gum. Add a shaker-full of ice to the blender, then blend until you have that perfect smoothie texture. Taste for sweetness and add the soluble sweetener to taste, then blend again.

Put the tapioca pearls, nata de coco or popping boba into the base of the serving glass and pour the smoothie blend over the top. Serve.

Or try this:

Try adding an extra ladleful of tapioca pearls on top before serving. The thickness of the iced blitz means the pearls will sit on the top of the drink as a garnish.

COCONUT ICED BLITZ

YOU WILL NEED:
- 100ml (3½fl oz) organic full-fat milk (or milk of your choice, see page 21)
- 30ml (2 tbsp) freshly brewed Jasmine tea
- pure coconut milk powder (check packet instructions for quantity, or to taste)
- ¼ tsp xanthan gum
- ice
- about 30ml (2 tbsp) soluble sweetener, such as agave syrup, cane syrup or Simple syrup (page 9), or to taste
- about 1 ladleful tapioca (page 10), nata de coco or popping boba

EQUIPMENT:
- blender
- 500ml (18fl oz) cocktail shaker
- 500ml (18fl oz) serving glass
- pea ladle
- bubble tea straw

Put the milk into the blender, along with the coconut milk powder, Jasmine tea and xanthan gum. Add a shaker-full of ice to the blender, then blend until you have that perfect smoothie texture. Taste for sweetness and add the soluble sweetener to taste, then blend again.

Put the tapioca pearls, nata de coco or popping boba into the base of the serving glass and pour the smoothie blend over the top. Serve.

Or try this:

Try using pure coconut milk instead of dairy milk and coconut milk powder in this recipe.

CREAM CROWN MATCHA

YOU WILL NEED:
- freshly brewed Jasmine tea (page 17), to fill
- ½ tsp pure matcha powder
- 100ml (3½fl oz) organic full-fat milk (or milk of your choice, see page 21)
- ice
- about 20ml (4 tsp) soluble sweetener, such as agave syrup, cane syrup or Simple syrup (page 9), or to taste
- about 1 ladleful tapioca (page 10) or caramelised tapioca (page 12)
- salted cream cheese crown (page 19)

EQUIPMENT:
- blender
- 500ml (18fl oz) cocktail shaker
- 500ml (18fl oz) serving glass
- pea ladle
- bubble tea straw

Put 50ml (2fl oz) freshly brewed Jasmine tea into the blender along with the matcha powder and milk and blend to combine.

Fill the shaker with ice and pour the matcha mix into it. Pour in some more Jasmine tea, if needed, to fill the shaker almost to the brim. Put the lid on and shake for a few seconds. Taste for sweetness and add the soluble sweetener to taste, then shake again.

Put your chosen tapioca pearls into the base of the serving glass and pour the contents of the shaker over the top, leaving a gap of about 2.5cm (1 inch) at the top of the glass. Top with the pre-made cream crown, which will float on top of the drink. Serve.

Or try this:

Turn this into a smoothie by adding ice and xanthan gum to the blender.

CHOCOLATE & HAZELNUT CREAM CROWN

YOU WILL NEED:
- freshly brewed Jasmine tea (page 17), to fill
- 2 tbsp chocolate and hazelnut spread
- 100ml (3½fl oz) organic full-fat milk (or milk of your choice, see page 21)
- ice
- about 1 ladleful tapioca (page 10) or caramelised tapioca (page 12)
- salted cream cheese crown (page 19)

EQUIPMENT:
- blender
- 500ml (18fl oz) cocktail shaker
- 500ml (18fl oz) serving glass
- pea ladle
- bubble tea straw

Put 50ml (2fl oz) freshly brewed Jasmine tea into the blender along with the chocolate and hazelnut spread and the milk. Blend to combine.

Fill the shaker with ice and pour the chocolate and hazelnut mix into it. Pour in some more Jasmine tea, if needed, to fill the shaker to the brim. Put the lid on and shake for a few seconds.

Put your chosen tapioca pearls into the base of the serving glass and pour the contents of the shaker over the top, leaving a gap of about 2.5cm (1 inch) at the top of the glass. Top with the pre-made cream crown, which will float on top of the drink. Serve.

ADVANCED MIXOLOGY

We highly recommend that you fully accustom yourself with the basic recipes in the prior sections before attempting the advanced bubble tea recipes in this section!

BANOFFEE PIE

YOU WILL NEED:
- freshly brewed Jasmine tea (page 17), to fill
- 100ml (3½fl oz) organic full-fat milk (or milk of your choice, see page 21)
- 1 small banana
- ice
- about 20ml (4 tsp) soluble sweetener, such as agave syrup, cane syrup or Simple syrup (page 9), or to taste
- about 1 ladleful tapioca (page 10) or caramelised tapioca (page 12)
- toffee syrup and whipped cream, to garnish

EQUIPMENT:
- blender
- 500ml (18fl oz) cocktail shaker
- 500ml (18fl oz) serving glass
- pea ladle
- bubble tea straw

Put 50ml (2fl oz) freshly brewed Jasmine tea into the blender along with the milk and banana. Blend to combine.

Fill the shaker with ice and pour the banana mixture into it. Pour in some more Jasmine tea, if needed, to fill the shaker almost to the brim. Put the lid on and shake for a few seconds. Taste for sweetness and add the soluble sweetener to taste, then shake again.

Put your chosen tapioca pearls into the base of the serving glass and drizzle toffee syrup around the inside of the glass, which will create a wonderful effect – don't be afraid to be generous! Pour the contents of the shaker into the glass and top with whipped cream and another drizzle of toffee syrup.

PINK
TEDDY

YOU WILL NEED:
- freshly brewed Jasmine tea
  (page 17), to fill
- handful of raspberries
- 100ml (3½fl oz) organic full-fat milk
  (or milk of your choice, see page 21)
- handful of shortbread biscuit (cookie)
  crumbs, plus extra to garnish
- ice
- about 20ml (4 tsp) soluble sweetener,
  such as agave syrup, cane syrup or
  Simple syrup (page 9), or to taste
- about 1 ladleful tapioca (page 10)
  or caramelised tapioca (page 12)
- whipped cream, to garnish

EQUIPMENT:
- blender
- 500ml (18fl oz) cocktail shaker
- 500ml (18fl oz) serving glass
- pea ladle
- bubble tea straw

Put 50ml (2fl oz) freshly brewed
Jasmine tea in the blender along with
the raspberries, milk and shortbread
crumbs. Blend to combine.

Fill the shaker with ice and pour the
blended pink teddy mix into it. Pour in
some more Jasmine tea, if needed, to
fill the shaker almost to the brim. Put
the lid on and shake for a few seconds.
Taste for sweetness and add the soluble
sweetener to taste, then shake again.

Put your chosen tapioca pearls into the
base of the serving glass and pour the
contents of the shaker over the top.
Garnish with whipped cream and more
shortbread crumbs.

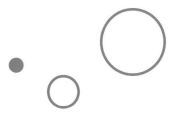

SPICED MANGO LASSI

YOU WILL NEED:
- 2 tbsp natural yogurt
- 100ml (3½fl oz) organic full-fat milk (or milk of your choice, see page 21)
- handful of diced fresh mango (or mango puree, to taste)
- freshly brewed Jasmine tea (page 17), to fill
- about 20ml (4 tsp) soluble sweetener, such as agave syrup, cane syrup or Simple syrup (page 9), or to taste
- ice
- 3 cardamom pods, lightly crushed, plus extra to garnish
- about 1 ladleful tapioca (page 10) or caramelised tapioca (page 12)

EQUIPMENT:
- blender
- 500ml (18fl oz) cocktail shaker
- 500ml (18fl oz) serving glass
- pea ladle
- bubble tea straw

Put the yogurt into the blender, along with the diced mango or mango puree and 30ml (2 tablespoons) freshly brewed Jasmine tea. Blend to combine.

Fill the shaker with ice and pour the blended mango lassi mixture into it. Pour in some more Jasmine tea, if needed, to fill the shaker almost to the brim, and add the cardamom pods. Put the lid on and shake for a few seconds. Taste for sweetness and add the soluble sweetener to taste, then shake again.

Put your chosen tapioca pearls into the base of the serving glass and pour the contents of the shaker over the top. Garnish with some more crushed cardamom pods.

STRAWBERRIES & CREAM

YOU WILL NEED:
- freshly brewed Jasmine tea
  (page 17), to fill
- 100ml (3½fl oz) organic full-fat milk
  (or milk of your choice, see page 21)
- handful of strawberries (or strawberry
  puree, to taste), plus extra to garnish
- about 20ml (4 tsp) soluble sweetener,
  such as agave syrup, cane syrup or
  Simple syrup (page 9), or to taste
- ice
- about 1 ladleful tapioca (page 10),
  caramelised tapioca (page 12) or
  popping boba
- whipped cream, to garnish

EQUIPMENT:
- blender
- 500ml (18fl oz) cocktail shaker
- 500ml (18fl oz) serving glass
- pea ladle
- bubble tea straw

Put 50ml (2fl oz) freshly brewed Jasmine tea into the blender along with the milk and strawberries or strawberry puree. Blend to combine.

Fill the shaker with ice and pour the blended strawberry mixture into it. Pour in some more Jasmine tea, if needed, to fill the shaker almost to the brim. Put the lid on and shake for a few seconds. Taste for sweetness and add the soluble sweetener to taste, then shake again.

Put your chosen tapioca pearls or popping boba into the base of the serving glass and pour the contents of the shaker over the top. Top with whipped cream and garnish with a few fresh strawberries.

Or try this:

You can also use any other berries of your choice instead of strawberries.

MINT CHOCOLATE WHIP

YOU WILL NEED:
- freshly brewed Jasmine tea
  (page 17), to fill
- 100ml (3½fl oz) organic full-fat milk
  (or milk of your choice, see page 21)
- 2 tbsp chocolate and hazelnut spread
- a few fresh mint leaves, plus extra
  to garnish
- ice
- about 1 ladleful tapioca (page 10)
  or caramelised tapioca (page 12)
- whipped cream and chocolate
  sprinkles, to garnish

EQUIPMENT:
- blender
- 500ml (18fl oz) cocktail shaker
- 500ml (18fl oz) serving glass
- pea ladle
- bubble tea straw

Put 50ml (2fl oz) freshly brewed Jasmine tea into the blender along with the milk, chocolate and hazelnut spread and mint leaves. Blend to combine.

Fill the shaker with ice and pour the blended chocolate and mint mixture into it. Pour in some more Jasmine tea, if needed, to fill the shaker to the brim. Put the lid on and shake for a few seconds.

Put your chosen tapioca pearls into the base of the serving glass and pour the contents of the shaker over the top. Top with whipped cream and garnish with chocolate sprinkles and fresh mint leaves. Serve.

Or try this:

- Try adding your favourite chocolate
  bar instead of the chocolate and
  hazelnut spread.

COOKIE CRUSH

YOU WILL NEED:
- freshly brewed Jasmine tea (page 17), to fill
- a few drops of vanilla extract (check packet instructions for exact quantity)
- 100ml (3½fl oz) organic full-fat milk (or milk of your choice, see page 21)
- handful of crushed chocolate cookies with vanilla filling, plus extra to garnish
- about 20ml (4 tsp) soluble sweetener, such as agave syrup, cane syrup or Simple syrup (page 9), or to taste
- ice
- about 1 ladleful tapioca (page 10) or caramelised tapioca (page 12)
- whipped cream, to garnish

EQUIPMENT:
- blender
- 500ml (18fl oz) cocktail shaker
- 500ml (18fl oz) serving glass
- pea ladle
- bubble tea straw

Put 100ml (3½fl oz) freshly brewed Jasmine tea into the blender along with the vanilla extract, milk and crushed chocolate and vanilla cookies. Blend to combine.

Fill the shaker with ice and pour the blended mixture into it. Pour in some more Jasmine tea, if needed, to fill the shaker almost to the brim. Put the lid on and shake for a few seconds. Taste for sweetness and add the soluble sweetener to taste, then shake again.

Put your chosen tapioca pearls into the base of the serving glass and pour the contents of the shaker over the top. Top with whipped cream and garnish with more crushed cookies. Serve with a dozen more cookies on the side!

Or try this:

Try swapping out the chocolate and vanilla cookies for your favourite kind of biscuit or cookie.

MERMAID

YOU WILL NEED:
- freshly brewed Jasmine tea (page 17), to fill
- pure coconut milk powder (check packet instructions for quantity, or to taste)
- 100ml (3½fl oz) organic full-fat milk (or milk of your choice, see page 21)
- natural blue food colouring (check packet instructions for quantity)
- ice
- about 20ml (4 tsp) soluble sweetener, such as agave syrup, cane syrup or Simple syrup (page 9), or to taste
- about 1 ladleful tapioca (page 10) or caramelised tapioca (page 12)
- edible gold dust, edible gold nuggets and pink iced ring-shaped biscuit (cookie)

For the strawberry whipped cream: (makes enough for up to 6 drinks)
- 240ml (8fl oz) whipping cream
- natural pink food colouring (check packet instructions for quantity)
- strawberry syrup, to taste

EQUIPMENT:
- whipped cream dispenser and chargers/cartridges
- blender
- 500ml (18fl oz) cocktail shaker
- 500ml (18fl oz) serving glass
- pea ladle
- bubble tea straw

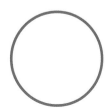

This drink requires two separate elements – the strawberry flavoured cream and the drink base. We did warn you that it will get more complicated as we go along!

To make the strawberry whipped cream, add the whipping cream, natural pink food colouring and strawberry syrup to the whipped cream dispenser and shake vigorously. Be sure to keep this mix constantly refrigerated and add the gas charger/cartridge to the whipped cream dispenser according to the manufacturer's instructions when you are ready to use it.

Put 50ml (2fl oz) freshly brewed Jasmine tea into the blender, along with the coconut milk powder, milk and natural blue food colouring. Blend to combine.

Fill the shaker with ice and pour the blended Mermaid mixture into it. Pour in some more Jasmine tea, if needed, to fill the shaker almost to the brim. Put the lid on and shake for a few seconds.

Taste for sweetness and add the soluble sweetener to taste, then shake again.

Put your chosen tapioca pearls into the base of the serving glass and pour the contents of the shaker over the top. Top with the strawberry whipped cream and decorate with the gold dust, gold nuggets and pink iced ring biscuit.

Phew! Now you have the hang of this, the Pixie (page 76) will be a breeze!

PIXIE

YOU WILL NEED:
- freshly brewed Jasmine tea (page 17), to fill
- a few drops of vanilla extract (check packet instructions for exact quantity, or to taste)
- 100ml (3½fl oz) organic full-fat milk (or milk of your choice, see page 21)
- 100ml (3½fl oz) lychee juice
- natural pink food colouring (check packet instructions for quantity)
- ice
- about 20ml (4 tsp) soluble sweetener, such as agave syrup, cane syrup or Simple syrup (page 9), or to taste
- about 1 ladleful tapioca (page 10) or caramelised tapioca (page 12)
- edible confetti and rainbow and unicorn decorations, to garnish

For the passion fruit whipped cream: (makes enough for up to 6 drinks)
- 240ml (8fl oz) whipping cream
- natural orange food colouring (check packet instructions for quantity)
- passion fruit syrup, to taste

EQUIPMENT:
- whipped cream dispenser and chargers/cartridges
- blender
- 500ml (18fl oz) cocktail shaker
- 500ml (18fl oz) serving glass
- pea ladle
- bubble tea straw

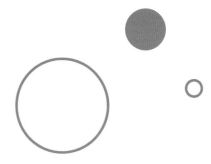

As before, this drink requires two separate elements – the passion fruit flavoured cream and the drink base.

To make the passion fruit whipped cream, add the whipping cream, natural orange food colouring and passion fruit syrup to the whipped cream dispenser and shake vigorously. Be sure to keep this mix constantly refrigerated and add the gas charger/cartridge to the whipped cream dispenser according to

the manufacturer's instructions when you are ready to use it.

Put 50ml (2fl oz) freshly brewed Jasmine tea into the blender, along with the vanilla extract, milk, lychee juice and natural pink food colouring. Blend to combine.

Fill the shaker with ice and pour the blended Pixie mixture into it. Pour in some more Jasmine tea, if needed, to fill the shaker almost to the brim. Put the lid on and shake for a few seconds. Taste for sweetness and add the soluble sweetener to taste, then shake again.

Put your chosen tapioca pearls into the base of the serving glass and pour the contents of the shaker over the top. Top with the passion fruit whipped cream and decorate with the edible confetti and rainbow and unicorn decorations.

GENIE

YOU WILL NEED:
- freshly brewed Jasmine tea (page 17), to fill
- a few drops of vanilla extract (check packet instructions for exact quantity, or to taste)
- handful of blueberries
- 100ml (3½fl oz) organic full-fat milk (or milk of your choice, see page 21)
- natural pink food colouring (check packet instructions for quantity)
- natural blue food colouring (check packet instructions for quantity)
- ice
- about 20ml (4 tsp) soluble sweetener, such as agave syrup, cane syrup or Simple syrup (page 9), or to taste
- about 1 ladleful tapioca (page 10) or caramelised tapioca (page 12)
- iced gem biscuits and edible confetti, to garnish

For the apple whipped cream:
(makes enough for up to 6 drinks)
- 240ml (8fl oz) whipping cream
- natural green food colouring (check packet instructions for quantity)
- apple syrup, to taste

EQUIPMENT:
- whipped cream dispenser and chargers/cartridges
- blender
- 500ml (18fl oz) cocktail shaker
- 500ml (18fl oz) serving glass
- pea ladle
- bubble tea straw

As before, this drink requires two separate elements – the apple flavoured cream and the drink base.

To make the apple whipped cream, add the whipping cream, natural green food colouring and apple syrup to the whipped cream dispenser and shake vigorously. Be sure to keep this mix constantly refrigerated and add the gas charger/cartridge to the whipped

cream dispenser according to the manufacturer's instructions when you are ready to use it.

Put 50ml (2fl oz) freshly brewed Jasmine tea into the blender, along with the vanilla extract, blueberries, milk, and natural pink and blue food colouring. Blend to combine.

Fill the shaker with ice and pour the blended Genie mixture into it. Pour in some more Jasmine tea, if needed, to fill the shaker almost to the brim. Put the lid on and shake for a few seconds. Taste for sweetness and add the soluble sweetener to taste, then shake again.

Put your chosen tapioca pearls into the base of the serving glass and pour the contents of the shaker over the top. Top with the apple whipped cream and decorate with the iced gem biscuits and edible confetti.

BLUE LYCHEE LATTE

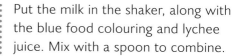

YOU WILL NEED:
- 130ml (4½fl oz) organic full-fat milk (or milk of your choice, see page 21)
- natural blue food colouring (check packet instructions for quantity)
- 30ml (2 tbsp) lychee juice
- about 1 ladleful tapioca (page 10)
- ice
- freshly brewed coffee, to fill
- soluble sweetener, such as agave syrup, cane syrup or Simple syrup (page 9), optional

EQUIPMENT:
- 500ml (18fl oz) cocktail shaker
- spoon
- 500ml (18fl oz) serving glass
- pea ladle
- bubble tea straw

Put the milk in the shaker, along with the blue food colouring and lychee juice. Mix with a spoon to combine.

Put the tapioca pearls into the base of the serving glass, then pour the milk and lychee mix over the top. Fill the glass three-quarters full with ice.

If you want to add soluble sweetener to your coffee, mix it in now.

Position a spoon about 1cm (½ inch) above the surface of the lychee and milk mixture. Slowly pour the coffee over the spoon and into the serving glass, raising the spoon as the liquid level rises to keep it the same distance above the liquid. This will ensure that the coffee hits the liquid below very gently, maintaining the separation between the coffee and the blue lychee milk and creating a beautiful visual effect.

PEANUT-LOADED FREAK

YOU WILL NEED:

- freshly brewed Jasmine tea (page 17), to fill
- 120ml (4fl oz) organic full-fat milk (or milk of your choice, see page 21)
- a few drops of vanilla extract (check packet instructions for exact quantity)
- 3 tbsp smooth peanut butter
- ice
- about 30ml (2 tbsp) soluble sweetener, such as agave syrup, cane syrup or Simple syrup (page 9), or to taste
- about 1 ladleful tapioca (page 10) or caramelised tapioca (page 12)
- whipped cream, mini peanut butter cups and chocolate-coated biscuit sticks, to garnish

EQUIPMENT:

- blender
- 500ml (18fl oz) cocktail shaker
- 500ml (18fl oz) serving glass
- pea ladle
- bubble tea straw

Put 60ml (4 tablespoons) freshly brewed Jasmine tea in the blender, along with the milk, vanilla extract and peanut butter. Blend to combine.

Fill the shaker with ice and pour the blended peanut mix into it. Pour in some more Jasmine tea, if needed, to fill the shaker almost to the brim. Put the lid on and shake for a few seconds. Taste for sweetness and add the soluble sweetener to taste, then shake again.

Put your chosen tapioca pearls into the base of the serving glass and pour the contents of the shaker over the top. Top with whipped cream and decorate with mini peanut butter cups and chocolate-coated biscuit sticks for an indulgent treat!

NOJITO

YOU WILL NEED:
- handful of fresh mint leaves
- ice
- 100ml (3½fl oz) lychee juice
- 50ml (2fl oz) freshly brewed Jasmine tea (page 17)
- coconut water, to fill
- about 1 ladleful tapioca (page 10), nata de coco or popping boba

EQUIPMENT:
- 500ml (18fl oz) cocktail shaker
- muddler
- 500ml (18fl oz) serving glass
- pea ladle
- bubble tea straw

Put the fresh mint leaves in the shaker and use the muddler to crush them. Fill the shaker with ice, then add the lychee juice and Jasmine tea. Pour in enough coconut water to fill the shaker to the brim. Put the lid on and shake for a few seconds.

Put the tapioca pearls, nata de coco or popping boba into the base of the serving glass and pour the contents of the shaker over the top.

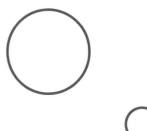

BUTTERFLY PEA
INFUSED LEMON FRUIT TEA

YOU WILL NEED:
- ice
- 250ml (9fl oz) freshly brewed Jasmine tea (page 17)
- 15ml (1 tbsp) butterfly pea flower extract
- about 1 ladleful tapioca (page 10), nata de coco or popping boba
- lemonade, to fill
- juice of ½ lemon

EQUIPMENT:
- 500ml (18fl oz) cocktail shaker
- 500ml (18fl oz) serving glass
- pea ladle
- spoon
- strainer
- bubble tea straw

Half-fill the shaker with ice, then add the freshly brewed Jasmine tea and the butterfly pea flower extract. Put the lid on and shake for a few seconds.

Put the tapioca pearls, nata de coco or popping boba into the base of the serving glass and add about 3 ice cubes. Pour 150ml (¼ pint) of the lemonade over the top. Add the freshly squeezed lemon juice and stir (this step is very important).

Position a spoon about 1cm (½ inch) above the surface of the lemonade. Slowly strain the liquid from the shaker into the glass, pouring it gently over the spoon (do not add the ice from the shaker). Raise the spoon as the liquid level rises. This will ensure the tea and butterfly pea flower mixture hits the lemonade very gently. As you pour, the drink will transform from dark blue to pink. Serve.

Why does the drink change colour?
This is all down to pH levels, as butterfly pea flower extract will change colour based on different levels of acidity.

The butterfly pea flower extract is naturally blue, but when the acidity changes, the colour will change to a purple or even to a bright pink!

BUBBLE TEA COCKTAILS & MOCKTAILS

Bubble tea can also form the base of a whole range
of delicious alcoholic and virgin bubble tea cocktails!
This section of the book will show you how to make both.

Bubble tea straws and pearls

You will find that traditional bubble
tea straws will be too big for some
cocktail glasses, so you can trim
the straw to the right length with a
pair of scissors.

We don't recommend using the
delicious caramelised tapioca with
these drinks, as it may add too
much sweetness and viscosity,
so use the standard tapioca.

GINGER BEER FLOAT

YOU WILL NEED:
– ice
– 30ml (2 tbsp) freshly brewed Assam tea (page 17)
– 20ml (4 tsp) apple juice
– squeeze of fresh lime
– 10ml (2 tsp) elderflower cordial
– about 1 ladleful popping boba or nata de coco
– ginger beer, to fill
– scoop of strawberry or vanilla gelato

EQUIPMENT:
– 500ml (18fl oz) cocktail shaker
– 300ml (½ pint) cocktail glass
– pea ladle
– strainer
– bubble tea straw, cut to length if necessary

Half-fill the shaker with ice. Add the freshly brewed Assam tea, apple juice, a squeeze of lime juice and the elderflower cordial. Put the lid on and shake for a few seconds.

Put the popping boba or nata de coco in the bottom of the cocktail glass and strain the contents of the shaker into the glass (do not add any ice). Top up with the ginger beer but be sure to leave some space at the top of the glass. Finish the drink by adding a scoop of strawberry or vanilla gelato on top and serve.

BLACKBERRY BLISS

YOU WILL NEED:
- a handful of blackberries, plus extra to garnish
- about 1 ladleful popping boba or nata de coco
- ice
- 50ml (2fl oz) freshly brewed Jasmine tea (page 17)
- lemonade, to fill
- sprigs of fresh rosemary, to garnish

EQUIPMENT:
- jug
- muddler
- 350ml (12fl oz) old fashioned or rocks glass
- pea ladle
- bubble tea straw, cut to length if necessary

Put the handful of blackberries in the jug and use the muddler to crush them. Then transfer the crushed blackberries to the bottom of the glass, and place the the popping boba or nata de coco on top.

Add ice to the glass, along with the freshly brewed Jasmine tea, then fill the glass to just below the rim with lemonade. Garnish with fresh blackberries and sprigs of rosemary.

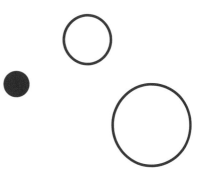

LAVENDER KISS

YOU WILL NEED:

- 80ml (2¾fl oz) organic full-fat milk (or milk of your choice, see page 21)
- 2 tsp dried edible lavender
- 30ml (2 tbsp) freshly brewed Jasmine tea (page 17)
- about 20ml (4 tsp) soluble sweetener, such as agave syrup, cane syrup or Simple syrup (page 9), or to taste
- ice
- about 1 ladleful tapioca (page 10)
- sprigs of lavender, to garnish

For the flower rim:

- edible flowers, chopped
- wedge of lime

EQUIPMENT:

- blender
- 500ml (18fl oz) cocktail shaker
- strainer
- 300ml (½ pint) cocktail glass
- pea ladle
- bubble tea straw, cut to length

To prepare the flower rim, scatter the flowers on a plate. Rub the lime wedge on the rim of the glass, then simply dip the edge of the glass into the flowers.

Put the milk in the blender along with the dried lavender and freshly brewed Jasmine tea. Blend to combine. Taste for sweetness and add the soluble sweetener to taste, then blend again.

Half-fill the shaker with ice and add the blended lavender mix. Put the lid on and shake for a few seconds.

Put the tapioca pearls in the cocktail glass, then strain the contents of the shaker into the glass (do not add the ice). Garnish with sprigs of lavender and serve.

DOWNTOWN DAQUIBERRY

YOU WILL NEED:
- small handful of raspberries (or raspberry puree, to taste), plus extra to garnish
- small handful of strawberries (or strawberry puree, to taste), plus extra to garnish
- 250ml (9fl oz) freshly brewed Jasmine tea (page 17)
- squeeze of lime
- ¼ tsp xanthan gum
- ice
- about 20ml (4 tsp) soluble sweetener, such as agave syrup, cane syrup or Simple syrup (page 9), or to taste
- about 1 ladleful popping boba or nata de coco

EQUIPMENT:
- blender
- 500ml (18fl oz) cocktail shaker
- 350ml (12fl oz) highball glass
- pea ladle
- bubble tea straw

Put the raspberries and strawberries (or purees) in the blender, along with the freshly brewed Jasmine tea, a squeeze of lime and the xanthan gum. Then half-fill the shaker with ice and add that to the blender too. Blend until you have that perfect smoothie texture. Taste for sweetness and add the soluble sweetener to taste, then blend again.

Put the popping boba or nata de coco in the glass and pour the smoothie mixture over the top. Top with fresh raspberries and strawberries and serve.

CLOUD NINE COFFEE

YOU WILL NEED:

- ice
- 120ml (4fl oz) freshly brewed black coffee
- 10ml (2 tsp) freshly brewed Assam tea (page 17)
- about 20ml (4 tsp) soluble sweetener, such as agave syrup, cane syrup or Simple syrup (page 9), or to taste
- about 1 ladleful tapioca (page 10)
- dark chocolate syrup, for drizzling
- coffee beans, to garnish

EQUIPMENT:

- 500ml (18fl oz) cocktail shaker
- 200ml (7fl oz) champagne coupe glass
- pea ladle
- strainer
- bubble tea straw, cut to length if necessary

Half-fill the shaker with ice. Add the black coffee and freshly brewed Assam tea. Taste for sweetness and add the soluble sweetener to taste. Put the lid on and shake until a froth develops.

Put the tapioca pearls in the bottom of the coupe glass and drizzle the dark chocolate syrup around the inside of the rim of the glass. Strain the contents of the shaker into the glass (do not add the ice), then top the drink with the foam from the shaker. Add some coffee beans on top to garnish.

BLACK RASPBERRY ROYALE

YOU WILL NEED:
– ice
– 60ml (2fl oz) whisky
– 25ml (1fl oz) raspberry liqueur
– dash of raspberry puree
– natural black food colouring (see packet instructions for quantity)
– 30ml (2 tbsp) freshly brewed Jasmine tea (page 17)
– ¼ tsp edible glitter
– about 1 ladleful popping boba

For the sugar rim:
– granulated sugar
– wedge of lime

EQUIPMENT:
– 500ml (18fl oz) cocktail shaker
– 300ml (½ pint) martini glass
– pea ladle
– strainer
– bubble tea straw, cut to length if necessary

To prepare the sugar rim, scatter some sugar on a plate. Rub the lime wedge on the rim of the glass, then simply dip the edge of the glass into the sugar.

Half-fill the shaker with ice. Add the whisky, raspberry liqueur, raspberry puree, black food colouring, freshly brewed Jasmine tea and edible glitter. Put the lid on and shake for a few seconds.

Put the popping boba into your prepared glass, then strain the contents of the shaker into the glass (do not add the ice). Serve.

THE BLUSHING DUCHESS

YOU WILL NEED:
– ice
– 50ml (2fl oz) vodka
– 25ml (1fl oz) triple sec
– 40ml (1½fl oz) cranberry juice
– 30ml (2 tbsp) freshly brewed
  Jasmine tea (page 17)
– squeeze of fresh lime
– ¼ tsp edible glitter
– about 1 ladleful popping boba
  or nata de coco

For the pink sugar rim:
– granulated sugar
– natural pink food colouring
– wedge of lime

EQUIPMENT:
– 500ml (18fl oz) cocktail shaker
– 300ml (½ pint) martini glass
– pea ladle
– strainer
– bubble tea straw, cut to length
  if necessary

To prepare the pink sugar rim, scatter some granulated sugar on a plate and add a small amount of pink food colouring. Mix until the sugar becomes pink (be sure not to dissolve the sugar). Rub the lime wedge on the rim of the glass, then simply dip the edge of the glass into the pink sugar.

Half-fill the shaker with ice. Add the vodka, triple sec, cranberry juice, freshly brewed Jasmine tea, a squeeze of fresh lime and the edible glitter. Put the lid on and shake for a few seconds.

Put the popping boba or nata de coco into the base of your prepared glass, then strain the contents of the shaker into the glass (do not add the ice). Serve.

THE MAJESTIC BUTTERFLY

YOU WILL NEED:

- 50ml (2fl oz) gin
- 2–3 drops of butterfly pea flower extract
- about 1 ladleful popping boba or nata de coco
- 150ml (¼ pint) premium tonic water
- squeeze of lime juice
- 30ml (2 tbsp) freshly brewed Jasmine tea (page 17)
- ice
- borage flowers, to garnish

EQUIPMENT:

- small glass
- spoon
- 350ml (12fl oz) highball glass
- pea ladle
- bubble tea straw

Before you begin the mixology, you will first need to infuse the gin. Simply pour the gin into a small glass and add 2–3 drops of the butterfly pea flower extract. Stir. The gin should change to an amazing deep blue colour.

The rest of this drink is made directly into the highball glass – there is no need for a shaker. First, put the popping boba or nata de coco into the glass. Pour over the tonic water and add a good squeeze of lime (this is very important) and the freshly brewed Jasmine tea. Add enough ice to fill three-quarters of the glass.

Now slowly pour the butterfly pea flower-infused gin into the glass and behold the colour change effect (see page 85 for an explanation). Garnish with borage flowers and serve.

TIKI PASSION

YOU WILL NEED:

– ice
– 50ml (2fl oz) rum
– 50ml (2fl oz) pineapple juice
– pulp of 3 fresh passion fruit
  (or passion fruit syrup, to taste)
– 30ml (2 tbsp) freshly
  brewed Jasmine tea (page 17)
– about 1 ladleful popping boba or
  nata de coco
– lime peel, to garnish

EQUIPMENT:

– 500ml (18fl oz) cocktail shaker
– 350ml (12fl oz) old fashioned
  or rocks glass
– pea ladle
– strainer
– bubble tea straw, cut to length
  if necessary

Half-fill the shaker with ice, then add the rum, pineapple juice, passionfruit pulp or syrup and freshly brewed Jasmine tea. Put the lid on and shake for a few seconds.

Put the popping boba or nata de coco into the glass, then strain the contents of the shaker into the glass (do not add any ice). Garnish with a spiral of lime peel and serve.

KOMBUCHA POMEGRANATE PUNCH

YOU WILL NEED:

– ice
– 80ml (2¾fl oz) kombucha
– 30ml (2 tbsp) freshly brewed Assam tea (page 17)
– ginger beer, to fill
– about 1 ladleful tapioca (page 10), popping boba or nata de coco
– fresh pomegranate seeds, lemon slices and mint leaves, to garnish

EQUIPMENT:

– 500ml (18fl oz) cocktail shaker
– 350ml (12fl oz) old fashioned or rocks glass
– pea ladle
– strainer
– bubble tea straw, cut to length if necessary

Half-fill the shaker with ice, then add the kombucha and freshly brewed Assam tea. Put the lid on and shake for a few seconds.

Put the tapioca pearls, popping boba or nata de coco into the glass, then layer on some fresh pomegranate seeds and lemon slices.

Strain the contents of the shaker into the glass (do not add any ice). Top up with the ginger beer, then garnish with fresh mint leaves and serve.

THE BIG CITY PUNCH

YOU WILL NEED:
– 25ml (1fl oz) vodka
– 25ml (1fl oz) triple sec
– 25ml (1fl oz) gin
– 25ml (1fl oz) white rum
– 40ml (1½fl oz) cranberry juice
– 30ml (2 tbsp) freshly brewed
  Jasmine tea (page 17)
– dash of peach syrup
– about 1 ladleful popping boba
  or nata de coco
– lemonade, to fill
– fresh sliced strawberries and
  lime wedges, to garnish

EQUIPMENT:
– 500ml (18fl oz) cocktail shaker
– 350ml (12fl oz) highball glass
– pea ladle
– strainer
– bubble tea straw

Half-fill the shaker with ice. Add the vodka, triple sec, gin, white rum, cranberry juice, freshly brewed Jasmine tea and a dash of peach syrup. Put the lid on and shake for a few seconds.

Put the popping boba or nata de coco into the highball glass, along with the sliced strawberries and lime wedges. Strain the punch mixture from the shaker into the glass (do not add the ice) until the glass is about two-thirds full. Top up with lemonade and serve.

THE DUKE OF NEW YORK

YOU WILL NEED:
- dash of mango syrup
- ⅓ shot glass popping boba
- 10ml (2 tsp) freshly brewed Jasmine tea (page 17)
- about 30ml (2 tbsp) tequila
- lime wedge, to serve

For the blue salt rim:
- table salt
- natural blue food colouring
- wedge of lime

EQUIPMENT:
- 60ml (2fl oz) shot glass

To prepare the blue salt rim, scatter some salt on a plate and add a small amount of blue food colouring. Mix until the salt becomes blue (be sure not to dissolve the salt). Rub the lime wedge on the rim of the glass, then simply dip the edge of the glass into the blue salt.

Now add the mango syrup to the bottom of the salt-rimmed shot glass, then gently add the popping boba.

Add the freshly brewed Jasmine tea, then top up the glass with the tequila. Serve with a lime wedge.

IRISH CREAM CARAMEL KISS

YOU WILL NEED:
- ⅓ shot glass tapioca pearls (page 10)
- 10ml (2 tsp) freshly brewed Assam tea (page 17)
- about 30ml (2 tbsp) Irish cream liqueur
- whipped cream and caramel sauce, to garnish

EQUIPMENT:
- 60ml (2fl oz) shot glass

Put the tapioca pearls in the bottom of the shot glass. Add the freshly brewed Assam tea and the Irish cream liqueur. Top with some whipped cream and a drizzle of caramel sauce for added flavour.

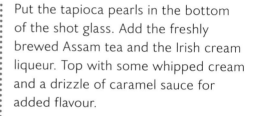

CREAM LIQUEUR CRUNCH

YOU WILL NEED:
- ⅓ shot glass tapioca pearls (page 10)
- 10ml (2 tsp) freshly brewed Assam tea (page 17)
- about 30ml (2 tbsp) marula cream liqueur
- double (heavy) cream and chopped nuts, to garnish

EQUIPMENT:
- 60ml (2fl oz) shot glass

Put the tapioca pearls in the bottom of the shot glass. Add the freshly brewed Assam tea and the cream liqueur. Layer on some double cream, then top with chopped nuts for garnish.

Ingredients glossary:

AGAVE SYRUP
A sweetener produced from several species of agave, including *Agave tequilana* and *Agave salmiana*. It's often used as an alternative to sugar or honey.

ASSAM TEA
A black tea produced in Assam, India. It is often used in breakfast tea blends and has a strong, robust flavour.

BORAGE FLOWER
Borage, also known as a starflower, is an annual herb in the flowering plant family *Boraginaceae*. The flowers are edible, with a sweet flavour, and make a great decoration for sweet drinks and desserts.

CALENDULA FLOWER
Yellow flowers, also known as marigolds. They can be eaten fresh or dried and make a colourful garnish as well as a tasty tea.

CARAMELISED TAPIOCA
This version of tapioca is cooked through a caramelisation process and is served warm (see page 12 for the recipe).

EDIBLE CONFETTI
Confetti-shaped sugar sprinkles that can be found in a variety of colours.

EDIBLE GLITTER
Shiny, sugar-based, food-safe glitter available in a variety of colours.

EDIBLE GOLD DUST
Food-safe gold dust for a shimmering finish.

EDIBLE GOLD NUGGETS
Small sweets the shape and colour of golden nuggets.

ELDERFLOWER CORDIAL
A cordial made from elderflowers and sugar. It has a sweet, floral taste.

ICED RING-SHAPED BISCUITS (COOKIES)
Ring-shaped biscuits with hard, colourful, crunchy icing.

IRISH CREAM LIQUEUR
A liqueur made with cream, Irish whiskey and cocoa.

JASMINE TEA
A delicate, fragrant tea, usually made with a green tea base scented with Jasmine blossoms. It is aromatic and slightly sweet.

MARULA CREAM LIQUEUR
A cream liqueur from South Africa. It is made with sugar, cream and the fruit of the African marula tree, giving it a fruity flavour.

MATCHA
A finely ground powder made from green tea leaves that have been specially grown and processed. It has a distinctive flavour and a bright green colour. It's usually prepared by whisking it into water or milk.

NATA DE COCO
A chewy jelly-like food made by fermenting coconut water.

PEANUT BUTTER CUPS
Chocolate cups containing peanut butter filling.

POPPING BOBA
Unlike tapioca, popping boba has a thin, gel-like skin with juice inside that bursts when squeezed. It's created using a spherification process and the outer shell of the popping boba is made with seaweed extract.

SOLUBLE SWEETENER
A sweetener that dissolves in water, such as agave syrup or cane syrup. See page 9 for our simple sugar syrup.

TAPIOCA
Tapioca pearls are black. They are made from cassava starch, with the addition of brown sugar for flavour. They have a chewy texture, and are synonymous with bubble tea.

TARO
A root vegetable from the tropical plant taro. It is used in desserts across the world. Taro can be used to flavour bubble tea, and has a slightly sweet, nutty taste.

XANTHAN GUM
An effective thickening agent, great for creating a perfect smoothie texture. It also works as a stabiliser, preventing ingredients from separating.

YUZU
A yellow citrus fruit that looks a little like a small grapefruit.

Equipment glossary:

BLENDER
An electric mixing machine used in food or drink preparation to mix ingredients or puree or liquidise food.

BUBBLE TEA STRAW
A large straw used in the consumption of bubble tea, which is wide enough for tapioca pearls, popping boba or coco de nata to be sucked through. You can find paper or reusable metal bubble tea straws online.

CREAM CHARGER/CARTRIDGE
A steel cylinder or cartridge filled with nitrous oxide. It is fitted to a whipped cream dispenser (see below) and serves as a whipping agent to instantly create light, airy whipped cream.

MUDDLER
A stick used to lightly mash cocktail ingredients and stir cocktails.

PEA LADLE
A ladle designed to drain one serving at a time. It's perfect for portioning out tapioca pearls as it helps easily control portion sizes to prevent wastage and ensure consistent presentation.

SOUP KETTLE
Also known as a soup warmer, this is a piece of kitchen equipment that keeps liquid foods, like soup, hot over a long period of time.

WHIPPED CREAM DISPENSER
A handheld piece of kitchen equipment that uses nitrous oxide gas to whip ingredients, which gives them a soft and pillowy texture.

INDEX

agave syrup 8, 108
apple juice 88
Assam tea 8, 17, 108
    cloud nine coffee 95
    cream liqueur crunch 107
    ginger beer float 88–9
    hot Assam tea 52
    hot ginger milk tea 48
    Irish cream caramel kiss 106
    kombucha pomegranate
      punch 102
    milk tea 24–5

banoffee pie 64–5
the big city punch 103
black raspberry royale 96–7
blackberry bliss 90–1
the blushing duchess 98
borage flower 108
Bubbleology 6
butterfly pea flower 84–5, 99

calendula flower 108
cane syrup 8
caramel frappe 42
caramelised tapioca 12–13, 108
Chai tea 38–9, 53
Chamomile tea 17
chocolate
    chocolate and hazelnut
      cream crown 60–1
    cloud nine coffee 95
    cookie crush 72–3
    milk chocolate whip 70–1
    sprinkles 108
    cocktails 96–103

coconut
    coconut iced blitz 58
    coconut milk tea 30–1
    mermaid 74–5
coffee
    blue lychee latte 80
    caramel frappe 42
    cloud nine coffee 95
cold bubble teas 22–45
cookie crush 72–3
cranberry juice 98, 103
cream cheese crown 18, 19,
    59, 60

downtown daquiberry 94
the Duke of New York 104–5

Earl Grey tea 17, 24
edible confetti/glitter/gold 74,
    108
elderflower cordial 88, 108
electric yuzu 36
equipment 109

flavour bases 20–1

genie 78–9
gin 99
ginger beer 24, 88
ginger juice 48

honey 8
hot milk teas 46–53

iced blitzes 56–8
Irish cream caramel kiss 106

Jasmine tea 8, 17, 108
    banoffee pie 64–5
    blackberry bliss 90–1
    butterfly-pea infused lemon
      fruit tea 84–5
    chocolate and hazelnut
      cream crown 60–1
    in cocktails 96–9, 103
    coconut milk tea 30–1
    cookie crush 72–3
    cream crown matcha 59
    downtown daquiberry 94
    the Duke of New York 104–5
    electric yuzu 36
    genie 78–9
    hot cocoa milk tea 49
    jasmine milk tea 28, 44–5
    lavender kiss 92–3
    the majestic butterfly 99
    mango fruit tea 34
    mango iced blitz 56–7
    matcha milk tea 29
    mermaid 74–5
    milk chocolate whip 70–1
    nojito 82–3
    passion fruit tea 32–3
    peanut-loaded freak 81
    and pineapple tea 43
    pink teddy 66
    pixie 76–7
    spiced mango lassi 67
    strawberries and cream 68–9
    strawberry fruit tea 35
    strawberry and mint
      fizz 40–1
    taro milk tea 26–7

kefir and pineapple tea 43
kombucha pomegranate
    punch 102

lavender kiss 92–3
lemonade
    blackberry bliss 90–1
    butterfly-pea infused lemon
        fruit tea 84–5
    electric yuzu 36
lychee juice
    blue lychee latte 80
    nojito 82–3
    pixie 76–7

the majestic butterfly 99
mango 34, 56, 67, 104
marula cream liqueur 107
matcha powder 29, 50,
    59, 108
measurements 21
mermaid 74–5
milk tea, coconut 30–1
milks 21
mint 70, 82
    strawberry and mint fizz 40–1
mocktails 88–95

nata de coco 14–15, 108
nojito 82–3

Oolong tea 17, 24

passion fruit 33, 101
peanut butter cups 108
peanut-loaded freak 81

pearls 10–15
    perfect tapioca pearls 10–11
pineapple juice 43, 101
pink teddy 66
pixie 76–7
popping boba 14–15, 109

raspberries 66, 94, 96
rum 100–1, 103

shakers 21
shots 104–7
simple syrup 8–9
soluble sweeteners 8–9, 109
spiced chai tea 38–9
strainers 17
strawberries 35, 68–9, 94
syrup, simple 8–9

taro milk tea 26–7
taro powder 109
tea base 16–17
tequila 104–5
tiki passion 100–1
triple sec 98, 103

vanilla 53, 73, 76, 78, 81
vodka 98, 103

whisky 96–7

xanthan gum 55, 56, 58,
    94, 109

yogurt 67
yuzu 36, 109

ACKNOWLEDGEMENTS

This publication is the culmination of a journey which began
with the opening of the first Bubbleology store in April 2011.
This journey would not have been a success without the help
of my fantastic team, the encouragement of my family and,
most importantly, the loyal customers who have supported
us over the years. I would also like to thank everyone at Ebury
for your help in bringing this book to life.

2

Published in 2020 by Ebury Press an imprint of Ebury Publishing,
20 Vauxhall Bridge Road,
London SW1V 2SA

Ebury Press is part of the Penguin Random House group of companies
whose addresses can be found at global.penguinrandomhouse.com

This edition published by Ebury Press in 2020

www.penguin.co.uk

A CIP catalogue record for this book is available from the British Library

Inside Page Design: Louise Evans
Cover Design: Small Dots
Photography: Joff Lee (except image on page 5, Tom Joy)
Mixologist: Kibria Khan
Food Stylist: Mari Williams
Prop Stylist: Faye Wears
Brand Design Coordinator: Mary Medrana

ISBN 9781529107197

Printed and bound: TBB, a.s. Slovakia

MIX
Paper from
responsible sources
FSC® C018179